STORIES I

For Joan
to remember
the Folk festival!
Tony Rekert

TONY REKERT

ISBN:
978-1-959303-25-1
First Amazon Edition

For Dolly Dobbyn

Contents

FOREWORD

Ever noticed how much you can say in just one sentence?

Like: Alice, the one with the codfish skiff in Port Alberni, got her foot caught on the edge of the hold door, wearin' one of their new type of orange gumboots that the Fisheries guys say you gotta wear now, (well, she had one on and one-off, when she fell,) and now she's off work for the whole rest of the season, and the only reason she was working in the first place was to get the money to buy her new roof (she needs a new roof, *bad,* that place is *collapsing,*) but she ain't got enough hours in, or days with the damn gumboots, or something, so, Now what: she supposed to pay for that new pin herself, on top of the roof?

All writing is bound by a sense of form, dictated more or less by time and space, whether a sentence, a laundry list, or an inaugural address: choose your form and adapt it to the time allowed.

You string a certain number of sentences together and see what you can do inside that space: all those syllables, the echoing of subterranean tonalities, urgent ungulation, intentional mouth-move.

As a writer looking for a form, inevitably, you encounter the one true theme, which is The Origin of Voice: follow *that.* You follow the origins of consciousness: birth-blind buds of baby-being, the need to speak, say something, anything: "...Urrgha....."

I thought of this form after long and careful counting of my toes: since they are My Toes, this is My Form. But I'm a noble fellow, and so I am giving My Form away free: to you, I turn over my toes.

I think of this writing as poetry, where the line length is dictated by breath. The punctuation helps the flow of breath, as does the layout and arrangement on the page; the line is over when you've given it as many breaths as it needs.

Tony Rekert
My Kitchen Table
October 31, 2022

CHAPTER ONE

It is sometime in early February. It is a Monday.

Nine o'clock in the morning.

A clear day, with sunlight in the far field.

The two new parrots in the cage on the back porch are eyeing me intently. They are waiting to hear the rest of this story.

To keep them relaxed and to get them accustomed to my voice, I am going to tell them everything that is sitting on my kitchen table today.

Here we have a little ceramic Mayan woman about four inches tall who has a large and friendly serpent curling up the side of her and wrapping around the top part of her head as she stands confidently, one hand on her hip. She is probably the most important piece on the table, but she is by no means the last:

A piece of bamboo filled with chopsticks;

An empty bottle of soda;

A tiny little useless calendar, bought in the market, with a pretty picture, but some of this year's months and some of last year's months stapled on;

An Anthology of American poetry;

A volume of STORIES IN TEN SENTENCES;

A book of matches;

An obsidian Olmec head, about four inches thick;

Various little bags: some from India, some from Mexico;

Two clear glass spice bottles with stoppered tops containing samples of volcanic gravel from inside Oaxacan rain-sticks;

A torn, old pocketbook: Henri Charriere;

A brown apple core;

One small red plastic ashtray: PIMMS;

A plump ceramic whistles the size of a football, shaped like a dinosaur, which blows only four notes, sounding like four different bottles being blown into;

A record album: Ruben Blades, which I borrowed from Humberto months ago and still have not returned;

A clear plastic water spray bottle;

A Dictionary: Websters paperback;

Some scissors;

A coffee mug: 1986 World Masters Surfing;

A matching pair of socks, which doesn't seem possible;

A lighter in a brass case;

A little pendant-sized stone mask, hand-carved, with a frog on the forehead, sitting on a little leather bag;

One dirty dish towel;

A little carved soapstone jar containing perfume;

And a hand-carved rosewood box, inlaid with brass, containing another little stone mask.

Do we see a theme here?

HOW TO TEACH A RIVER TO WRITE

Suddenly the door opened: in walked a statue-perfect woman with a large snake on her head. No, too abrupt; make it more gradual.

One day, the river swelled up and overflowed its banks and flooded the whole area where the tree shrews were constructing their labyrinths...; oh, damn: I forgot to mention the labyrinths. Suddenly the door opened: I liked that part; the story was doing fine up to there.

Suddenly the door opened, and in marched the River, vocabularies astrew and niceties asunder, demanding to know the time.

When a river asks you the time, as you know, it is no frivolous matter, and of course, there is only one appropriate answer to be uttered immediately, which is to say,

NOW!

When? says the river.

NOW NOW NOW, you reply;

NOW and NOW and NOW.

Oh God, says the river;

I love it.

(NOW is the one-word rivers love to hear.)

CHAPTER THREE

Now, before we proceed, perhaps we should agree on some background: there are three images to keep in mind.

First is the image of rain upon the water: it is raining, water falling upon the water, and the individual raindrops pock the candle wick wet fat drops plop.

And so begins the spreading out of circles.

Perhaps we are standing on a float, a dock, by the edge of the sea, with huge firs and thrusty cedars leaning evening one side, and only ocean on the other, and the rain charging down, yahooing onto tin roofs and 45-gallon drums and onto you, onto you especially, ecstatic gum-boot face thrust trust-up, charging flowers, rushing urgent vocabularies from sea to living liquid air.

Second, we have the sound of Raven's wing: you can always tell Raven from Crow by the WHOOSH WHOOSH WHOOSH. Not to mention the voice: Crow is up, higher in the throat, resonating up the nasal passages, a hard wind. Raven is more back in the throat, more deeply seated, like someone who has been thinking about something for a long time and then begins to speak.

Three: what have we? Only this moment, only this one,

where you and I are,

now.

Sweet.

ON SPEAKING WITH A FORKED TONGUE

Someone is talking to you but not saying what they mean, or not saying what they mean to say, or not meaning what they say. You feel like a pilot buzzing a little airplane around the control tower, waiting for permission to land, waiting to find a way in, while the voice, spilling words, holds you away.

Behind the blind meringue, you can tell we're not there yet. There's something else being said here.

Knives, eyes, when they feel like it.

They say the word is mightier than the machine gun, but I'm not sure. I think it is the word not said, the thought raw-trapped and sprung behind articulate lying eyes that is more destructive: the one that destroys your bones.

The un-done ones undo you; the unsaid unsay.

There is no room on the runway.

We don't recognize your numbers.

CHAPTER 88 (for Bill W.)

The sun was roaring through the trees, blinding and hurtling me back through time, past Attila, past Genghis.

Such a sun once signaled a surge of harness, the charge of armored horses, and the intentional breathing machinery of war on foot with spears, swords, and clubs.

Meadows, especially, were good ground for a killing.

I took a sword in the mouth.

How the horses suffered.

Swinging back past Africa, where sun-born pygmies bake the sun anew each year in a special clay dish so that you and I might continue to enjoy the daylight.

Today the sun is never quite as bright as that, and there are very few pygmies left who remember.

Reaching even further back, we cruise the plain of pain, the burning world of raw red rock, which only the dinosaurs remember.

In such a time was a fire in the sky.

Now in late January, in the late millennium, late civilization, the sun is thin:

Little we see in Nature that is ours.

ON LOVE AND BEETLES

When a little South-American Green-Backed Beetle climbs up on top of another Green-Backed Beetle and begins to copulate with it, we do not call it Love; we call it Beetle.

However, when a person watches the Beetles for many years, dying to know what makes them Beetle, we call that Love: I Love my work.

But wait, you burble, thundering muskets askew on oaken caskets: ain't that just curiorskity?

Well, maybe that's all Love is when you get right down to it: curiosity.

Oh, go on, and Peshaw on such ramblings, you frown.

Consider the cat with the ball of yarn; the dog with the phonograph. The man with the woman.

To love is to know.

Marriages die when there is nothing left to know.

Beetle.

ON LOVE AND PIZZA

There are only two things essential to any form of civilized life and cultured human behavior: love and pizza.

Both make the world go round. And, in a pinch, if you've got to choose, you can get by on just pizza.

Oh, of course, not forever, but just until, just until Love comes stumbling your way again, that blind horse in your kitchen, until then.

Meanwhile, pizza.

Pizza fills up just about 95% of the holes carved inside of you by fear and loneliness, and the despair of old address books, and you can take a piece home with you and plug another hole in the morning.

There is something about pizza that impinges on Buddha-hood. Go on, ask any Buddha: Hey, Buddha, while I'm up, you want me to get you some *Love* or some *Pizza*?

They'll take Pizza every time. Look at their tummies; you never see a skinny Buddha.

CODFISH AT THE MARKET

Remarkably, little Billy was unscathed by his encounter with the codfish.

But the image of the ant-hill stayed with him: just there, beside the trail, looking like its own little wasteland, and one step closer, and you realize the whole area is alive with intentional activity, astonishing purpose, and precision, construction of Mayan labyrinths, with secret Queens and passwords.

The password, in this case, had been interred with their bones. Ants have bones, you know, but they are very tiny and instantly become very brittle upon death; therefore, they are very difficult to study: not many pet hospitals have fixed broken ants' legs yet.

Ah, but then, nobody knew that business about the butterflies, either, until just very recently; when was it, 1956?

The Aztecs knew it, of course: they released butterflies from their temples on the tops of pyramids, but then they forgot how to do it about 700 A.D., and nobody remembered again until just the other day, only now, of course, the butterflies are all gone, or just about, compared with how it was then, and anyway, such knowledge doesn't really have much practical value.

The same is apparently true of jellyfish: they share a kind of membrane through the pulse of an ocean that moans mucous music.

All of us have many membranes: getting to know someone is watching the layers of intricate membranes shift, slide, and re-arrange.

Of course, we cannot see our own membranes: we feel bare-skinned and naked before the juicy eyes.

Poke a finger at a fish at the market: COD.

CHAPTER TEN

So she stood there in the doorway, with this huge snake coiled up one side of her body and resting its head on the top of her head.

I believe I have mentioned the doorway before: framed with hand-carved posts representing visionary creatures in gardens, carved in Michoacan, Mexico.

Wait a minute.

Oh shit, I think I lost myself.

Let me see now..........

It's not so much that she has a snake on her head that is disturbing; it is rather that the two of them look so relaxed and natural together, as if you would expect to see such a thing every day.

You can't tell if one is the master of the other. It certainly doesn't seem to be a conventional relationship.

Then there is the matter of the skull at the woman's belt. This is not a woman to trifle with.

WHERE WERE WE

But we should do something with this woman standing in the doorway. We can't just leave her there; it would be rude. She's getting tired, I think, and perhaps a little exasperated: she wants to get on with this novel.

I can never write the word novel without thinking of the word navel, and then in turn of my grandmother's story about the retired Commander from the Royal Navy who was recognized from his lapel pin by another Commander who said, "I see you're Naval, sir." The first guy replies, "Oh, I beg your pardon," and tucks in the front of his shirt.

I suppose what makes the story funny is to realize what was funny for my grandmother in her time.

Therefore there are two levels to the humor, not to mention two levels to the word naval - for me, at least: for you, maybe not.

Maybe the word *naval* leaves you cold and flat as a dead flounder, whereas the word *iniquity*, let us say, or *boisterousness* reverberates for you like hot pancakes falling from the sky.

This makes me wonder how we ever actually succeed in communicating with one another, what with all these denotations and connotations and whiz-bang association airplanes caroming out of each syllable.

Quite a business.

ON WRITING STORIES IN TEN SENTENCES

It is not possible to write stories in ten sentences, nor is there any merit in attempting.

You always end up with more than ten or fewer than ten and have to lie with the punctuation; either you string a whole bunch of perfectly nice little sentences together into one long sentence, wobbling with semicolons and concatenating participles, or else you prune one nicely-fruited sentence into several nondescript and needlessly emphatic sound-bites.

It is an inherently ludicrous undertaking. Not only is it not possible: it is inherently senseless and possibly dangerous, contributing to the development of a diseased imagination. If we all sat around constructing Stories in Ten Sentences all day, who would mind the peas and carrots?

Who is minding them now, as far as that goes? It doesn't go very bloody far, does it?

So you see what I mean about this form: it is devious and spurious and flaming with envy.

That's not what I meant to say; that's not it at all.

(Shakes his head.)

SADDLE UP YOUR PARROTS

Did I ever tell you about the time I turned a sad man's saddles into parrots? It started with these two saddles Sad Jim gave me to sell for him if possible.

He was at the time going through his first million-dollar bankruptcy, splitting up his wife of twenty years and the kids and their home and the cars, and the furniture, and the (ahem) credit cards, and now these boxes of tennis racquets and curling brooms, and these two saddles, was pretty much all that was left over. He figured that since I sold poetry and silver jewelry and singing bowls at markets in the summertime, well, maybe I could offer these saddles for sale too.

I did like the look, the *leather* of them, and I had never really handled a saddle before, so I kept them for a while, took them with me in the van for a couple of trips, and showed them to a few people. The saddles seemed very happy to travel, although I could never get used to the red of the saddle blankets.

Then one day, I was thumbing through the local paper and saw an ad that said WANTED TO TRADE: TWO PARROTS FOR SADDLES.

So I went up there and met these people, and their kid, and their huge Weimaraner wearing a blanket, and their black hog in mud, and their twenty-six-year-old dwarf horse with thistles in its hair, and never mind the miniature ponies that were around somewhere, and this falling-over house, and five poodles in the kitchen, and a couple of cockatiels on the kitchen chair, and a half dozen finches on the counter, and, oh yes: these two parrots.

These folks had lived here for about ten years, only now they were going to sell it: they had a sign out front and everything, and they were going to move up to the Sunshine Coast and hopefully buy more land than this, this was only one acre, and anyway, be near her mom, and, sure, they really liked sad Jim's saddles.

Oh, you already heard that story: O.K., sorry.

CRAZY HORSE DEATH

Seems like it is the corny people who always get the good lines. You know, the people with teeth missing, wearing clothes that look just found.

These corny people, who tend to be from Dewdney, or Rock Creek, or just up behind Grand Forks there, take the third dirt road under the powerline: these people, outside of the reach of the big-city news media, all experience outrageous calamities as part of their every-day life.

They seem to develop the capacity for attracting the most preposterous calamities: their kid dies after being stepped on by a horse when their father was adjusting the saddle, but he had the torch on because he was brazing a horseshoe, so the horse catches on fire.

Or, this cool old innocent painter guy helps his thirty-four-year-old waitress sweetheart burn down a historic hotel, in Fort Langley, as a special favor, but then she runs off with the boss after they collect the insurance and buys a big house in Calgary.

But then, of course, the insurance says that they won't pay because there is no mention in the policy of saddles, or burned abandoned lovers, or something, and the guy is so frustrated he punches a policeman; he wouldn't ordinarily do that, you could ask anybody, he was a peaceful guy, but I mean come on, you know: this was my kids...

The policeman gets the other kids who were all asleep in their beds and puts them in the back of the paddy wagon and leaves them there shivering and scared with no blankets and crying while he goes off to investigate the smoldering scene; and meanwhile, the squawky police radio in the paddy wagon calls for an ambulance to pick up a dead kid under a burning horse.

On the day of the funeral, they cut off the telephone.

But I know it's all right because I just ask my baby in the sky; if my baby doesn't like who I am talking to, well, then I just clam right up.

I pretend I'm ignorant.

THE FIRST THING I WAS THINKING

A car went by: it gave me a reprieve; I didn't have to think about anything because I could just observe the car. Now, of course, the car is gone already, but here I am still writing about it.

Does that mean I'm thinking about it? I guess so. I could stop writing about it and continue thinking about it, however, I can't continue writing about it and stop thinking about it. So, it is a lop-sided relationship.

Speaking about lop-sided relationships, did I ever tell you about a guy I knew who had these huge heavy lips, like a halibut or a big codfish, only he never spoke a word - his wife did all the talking?

Oh, I did.

That's right, his name was Walter.

Oh, well, anyway, I guess I should tell you something else.

GAZING INTO FIRE

Those moments spent gazing into the fire: remember them?

Didn't there use to be more of them?

The little molten ships colliding in there, writhing crimson negatives of themselves, sliding shut with fiery eyes and molten mouths, opening, breathing with the pass of air upon them.

Or blown by you, purse-lipped; careful not to blow the ash. Just blow on the coals, lightly: that glowing piece of coal remembers when it was a tree, shelving off the patterns first laid down by veins and stems and ancient water-ways, aqueducts.

And how you could grab a stick and poke the log; turn it over like turning over a rock at the sea-shore to see what's under there, wiggling, hurrying things: so the coals begin to throb, exposed by you, so rudely, so intimately.

What's in here?

Why so familiar?

It feels at home.

Gazing into the fire.

THINGS WIND CAN SAY

As she got older, my grandmother used to complain about the noises in her head: Oh, she said, sometimes the noises are terrible. The only way to make them acceptable was to make them fit into some appropriate background.

She said it was like a river, a tremendous river rushing by beside you, with the big wind whooshing the leaves awash in summer aspen, birch: poplars plashed in the silver splash.

Once there was a man there, she said, shyly, have I told you, and two boys also: standing among the trees on the other side of the river. I could just make out their shapes of them there.

Then the two little boys came closer; in fact, soon they were standing right here beside my bed, she said, pointing from the side of her bed. I had my glasses off and my eyes half-shut, but I was not asleep; I guess they thought I was asleep.

They leaned right over my bed. I could feel the weight of them pressing against the side of the bed.

They liked me; it made them happy to look at me.

ON MAKING MUSIC: Part One

In our culture, we don't make music: we put it on.

In most other countries, at least away from cities, people make music themselves: hand-clapping, dancing, singing, tapping boxes, clicking sticks, shaking shells.

Perhaps that's true of 'underdeveloped' countries: people are more likely to make music the less 'developed' they are.

They couldn't whistle the opening bars of Mozart. They haven't been to see Kiri Te Kanawa lately.

But give a kid in Cuba two pencils, and he'll tap you out a Rhumba, and sing along on top of it while continuing to talk to you. The hills of Burma invoke ancient atonal arpeggios on bits of bamboo. Sorry, I'm getting carried away.

It must be all this racket.

Yak bells, random clank and bonk, at 17,000 feet: May in Mongolia.

ON MAKING MUSIC: Part Two

Yeah, so you can sing some songs, you know all the words, but how often do you sing? When was the last time you sang on the street, for instance, or in Safeway? In Senegal, you might, or Togo.

I stood on a little crowded ferry in Brazil while a woman I had just met two minutes ago stood right in front of me and sang loudly and passionately to me, straight into my face, with all her heart, in a language I did not speak, a whole song she had just written, which she felt contained a very important message to share because it was about what men and women really want from each other, while the crowd bumped and laughed and shouted around us, and guys with trays of cheese on their head elbowed past, while a caged TV played Soccer, and blind people played the accordions.

We sing at people's birthdays, the same song, and everybody all together, once, and then we're finished, and now blow out the candles and Let's eat that cake!

I was on a crowded subway in Mexico City. A very calm, dignified threadbare man about sixty years old gets on, stands for a moment, and as the door slides shut behind him, explains calmly to anyone who can hear, over the hum of motion and rocketing tunnels, that he used to have a job. Still, now he cannot work anymore because he has rheumatoid arthritis. His hands are crippled (he holds them up, and yes, they are poor withered branches...), so he is going to sing a song for us instead.

He hangs onto a pole with one gentle bent hand, and sings a love song from old 1940 black and white movies that you still see on television (first one sweet, melodious little verse, and then a rocketing pause of clattering wheels in tunnels, and then one more tender verse,) then he limps and squeezes his way down the length of the subway car, holding out his little can for pesos: *Gracias, senor.*

THE MULTI-RES MARLBORO MAN

Stood on the tiny front-street porch on the rainy night of a crowded house party in east Vancouver, out to have a cigarette, while this tall black guy, who told me he was a true baritone bass, tried to sell me part of a multi-residential condominium deal in St. Louis, Missouri.

The numbers were all there, ready, waiting to emerge, poking their heads above the water of his apparently random chatter to stand shimmering against the back-lit blackboard of the wet night.

This is just the first step for one building, he says.

The building has been appraised at between seven hundred thousand and nine hundred thousand dollars [BING!], but our company bought it at auction for three-hundred forty-four thousand [BING!], which means immediate equity for us of almost six hundred thousand dollars [BIG BING!]

His normal investors are too shy of this deal because they just can't believe it could be this good!

All you have to do is pay $80,000; then, in just a few months, virtually immediately, you get back $60,000, which is shared equally with the three other investors.

In five years, you get your full $80,000 back: the company will buy you out, giving you back every penny of your original investment.

All this in the time it took him to smoke a Marlboro.

A tall baritone money-funnel.

Eighty thousand: The Marlboro's on the house.

BRENDA AND THE BOOGEY MAN

Brenda first heard about the Boogey Man when she was three, and it chilled her blood. She heard it from Janice, who lived next door and was two years older than her, and for years after that, whenever she met somebody named Janice, she flinched.

When she was five, she used to tell stories about the Boogey Man and draw ferocious pictures of Him Looming Purple Teeth.

By the time she was seven, she could terrify her little sister until they hugged each other's knuckles white.

But now here she was; she wasn't little any more.

Drawings of stick men drew foreign as caves.

What name, what name to give, then,

to the relentless stack

of unfinished days,

this angry bathtub?

What name for sighs escaping

the morning's inevitable mist?

What name the shadow beneath the bed?

What name this?

ABOUT IMAGINARY CONVERSATIONS

I sometimes think I have more imaginary conversations than real ones.

I think that maybe the most meaningful conversations that people have are played out over and over again afterwards: repeat performances in the theatre of the head.

It is a good idea to know interesting people, because then, even when they are not there, you can continue to have interesting conversations. If you are the sort of person who may be prone to having imaginary conversations from time to time (sometimes spilling out, just a bit too loud, in the vegetable section, it looks like you are talking to the onions, you know what I mean, it happens to all of us, perfectly natural,) you might just as well have interesting ones.

Pretty bleak to imagine a person spending a lot of time having imaginary conversations with people that were boring: find yourself talking about dirt, for example, on and on and on and on, the way dirt gets into the house, and the type of dirt under your fingernails, the sheer number of microbes in your kitchen sink.

Oh, Christ, there's mud, you know, and footprints, and whole casual clomps of compost; and on the other end of the scale, there are microscopic colonies thriving, expanding, claiming new territories, big enough you can see them expanding, if you... if you get down on your knees, here, and take a look, See?

Especially the drools beneath the corners of the stove, behind the sink, or in dark little enclosures that nobody remembers. A mangle of mosses, jam-jungled blooms of bacteria blithely bestrewing the bottoms of your basins.

To have such a conversation for, let us say, weeks at a time, day in and day out, gazing at the floor, muttering, speculating . . .

Could prove to be

Injurious to one's health

After a time.

Let's talk about something else.

ON BEING A TOURIST

Strange how we spend long periods of time - weeks, months, years, lifetimes - waiting for a moment of significance, longing for a time when we can act the way we 'really' want to act and be the person we want to be; planning all year, saving for that trip to Fiji, to Barbados, to Spain, to the Galapagos, to Indonesia; there I will be happy; there my life will have new meaning.

And sure enough, we get to that place, and each moment seems magical, charged with significance; we penetrate the ordinary movements of someone else's day, fascinated to observe how they do ordinary things like cook food, build houses, and make beds, and say hello to one another; how they make love.

Yet those people do all those things, and they think, in turn: oh, if only I could be somewhere else, or someone else, in some other place, in some other time than this.

If I could travel to some far-off land, even for a little while, like Germany, Norway, America or Canada.... then, then I would know what it really means to be alive.

Two weeks, three weeks, a month would be wonderful: each day rich and fat and full; to wake up happy with the sounds there, to gaze at the things there are to gaze upon.

We come back home and fall into the inevitable dreary routine again; in two or three weeks, we're not really sure if we did those things at all, or if we just read about them, or saw them on television, or on somebody else's Instagram.

Then suppose somebody that you met in some village comes to visit you, comes to spend some time with you; for them, your ordinary day would be wonderful, mysterious, and exciting.

They find it all so interesting, how you open a tin of cat food, how you make toast, how you turn on the washing machine, how you mow the lawn, all the stupid ordinary things that drive you crazy.

And it comes to you that if you could see your day through the eyes of a stranger, then you wouldn't have to travel half-way round the world and spend ten thousand dollars in order to find things interesting.

You could enjoy everything around you and savor the pleasure of being a tourist: a tourist in your own home.

MORE ON BEING A TOURIST

In Pago Pago, it is interesting to do the dishes: the dishes look different, for one thing, and they make a different sound when you stack them.

There are no washing machines there, and nobody seems to mind; they hang the clothes to dry outside on the palm-leaved verandah.

When you get back home, there is no romance to your laundry or your dishes; they just pile up there, by the sink, or around the house in various positions of despair.

To stop on the street in Mexico City and buy some fresh-squeezed juice in a plastic bag, or even just a bottle of water, brings you solace, a sense of relief and satisfaction, which seems impossible to obtain in your own country.

Why should this be? Why should we have to violate the skies with jet fuel and pay thousands of dollars in order to fly to another part of the world to enjoy a glass of water?

Surely it would be possible to obtain the same pleasure at your own corner store, or even at your own kitchen sink, for that matter.

But no: at home, we're pissed off with the sink and with the guy who runs the corner store; he wants 12 cents too much for milk, and he doesn't really care about you; he sees you every day, and anyway he doesn't even speak your language properly.

The challenge is to be a tourist in your own back yard, in your own country, in your own kitchen, to receive each moment as a gift, with its rich fullness.

After all, no matter where you are, no matter how exotic the surroundings, still there is only this moment, this particular moment, to enjoy; this moment where the total stretch of space and time intersects:

here;

now;

you.

DEAR LONE RANGER

DEAR LONE RANGERr:

THIS iS silver. Hi. I'm tyPING With my hhoof. So sill haf ta be Short. And I'm onley allowit ten sentiss. Jest wANTET TO let you know i love you.

NO HARd feILLINGS ABOUT THE SADDIL.

I understnd. Not even THE Bridle. It was meant to bE.

Silverr.

TEN FOR MEXICO CITY

Sweet, terrible beauty: Gods clogged with smog; legless kings on corners selling ballpoint pens; pyramids in the subway.

On television every Saturday afternoon, old black and white movies with singing cowboys, Pedro Infante, Courtly Love.

In Mexican Soap Operas, people live in elaborate haciendas and own clean clothes with nice buttons. Always, of course, they yearn for love, proper love, and a statement of love from the chaste, unrelenting maidens: *No,* says one, turning her head: *the first time I kiss a man will be on the day I take my wedding vows.*

(And is that also the last time, I wonder, sitting with my love between two aunts, deaf Grandpa and a dozen dozing poodles: does it stop then?)

Meanwhile, outside, every third car is a white and yellow VW Taxi with the front seat removed: anywhere in the city, five bucks. *Yes, señor, I own dees car for nine years,* he says proudly; *third engine, 600,000 km, ees steel origin'l interior.*

Nine years also I have been here, says the giggly little shoe-shine man at the subway entrance, rubbing my shoes with his bare hands: *Before that, I was a vendredor ambulante; it was more difficult.*

A little kid about six years old gets on the subway, stands solemnly in position in front of the racketing door, sings at the top of his lungs, with great seriousness and authority, and then looks calmly around for anyone to offer him money. *Gracias, senor.*

THE SOLUTION TO ROADS

Once upon a time, all rivers ran the same way, which was always the direction you wanted to go.

It was easy, in those days, to go to all kinds of different places, although it was difficult to come back.

Then somebody invented roads. Roads are much better, they said; now you go, and you can come back again just as easily, no longer tied to rivers.

In fact, they dug up some of the rivers, put roads there, and turned the rivers around to make them fit, so now rivers ran the wrong way or didn't run at all.

For people who still preferred to travel by rivers, life became very confusing. Now it could be really difficult to come back from somewhere, but impossible to get there in the first place.

Practical people, however, soon mastered roads.

And the solution to roads was roads.

And the solution to more roads was more roads.

BARGAINS

Accusation in the eyes
Of barefoot Indian girls selling wind chimes,
Holding them in front of me like a gate.
They're only a dollar.
You don't have one dollar?
Sure I have a dollar,
But I don't want wind chimes;
They are hard to pack.
They break.
They are only a dollar; do you like?
Yes, I like.
Buy three.
Three?
Special price.

ON NOTHING

Anyhow the walls lean in at crazy angles, or was that angels, and vibrate, so how can you be sure.

You say to yourself, I guess something is happening here.

I think I know.

There, that tumult of walls and neon eyes; I'll have it fixed in a jiffy, but no, I, uh, I mean . . ., nothing.

(Sunlight through the window:

A spot of sun on the grass.

Brrrr.

It's chilly.

A dog barks.

In the far field,

Wind.

(Shhhhhhhh..............)

CIRCLES

The wheels, the little circles:
A dog comes to lie down,
Curls in a circle, spirals down
Into sleep.
Flaming asteroids charge by very close
Every fifty thousand years or so.
Steam from the kettle;
Smoke. The lazy kind of natural way
That motion seems to take you,
Any motion.
All these things and more I have
Been thinking of saying
To you, rehearsing, speaking them
Out loud sometimes alone
Or in the garden, or asleep,
Almost asleep,
Just to get the words ready.
Mental pruning: Don't forget that one.
Snip snip, heh-heh.
(I remember.)
And the order of the years falls away from you,
Shedding stars and trees, dreams and streams and

Feathered dresses.
Snakes slough dry skin
And grow
Young again, again
You are,
You are young you,
Another moment.

THE WITNESS

Well, it was a snake, of that I am fairly certain, writhing lewdly shrewdly there.

On the ground, beneath the tree: in the shadows.

It was hard to see.

At first, I thought it was the ground itself moving, up-tumbling loamy smoke.

But it was him, snake, sure enough, the coily one: shining shoulders, fires and diamonds, emerald eyes: moving without moving.

And she came upon him there: firm-limbed, full-fleshed: She.

She sang to him, or so they say, or so it seemed; I couldn't catch the language somehow.

Waters flowing maybe making wingling wind-babies, sound of falling, feathers fondling, deeply calling creatures falling drowzy half-asleep.

Snake knew.

She knew too.

NORMA'S STORY

So anyways, let me tell you what happened.

I was driving, this was in Windsor, and we were just coming up to the last turn-off on our way to meet Beatrice's kids, Patrick and Lanny, who were up to see their mother for the long weekend, their Columbus Day or something; nice kids, they were staying with us.

I swear I didn't even touch the brake or anything; all I know is, well, I didn't know anything because I was unconscious when most of it happened, or, well, anyways, let me tell you what happened.

There was a guy coming up awful close behind me in the mirror, and he kind of bumped me, and my car went right off the road and did a complete three-sixty and landed on the roof.

Well, everybody was all right except me; they had to put me on a stretcher and take me to the hospital.

I woke up for a minute; I guess I thought I was dreaming or something, for they said I pawed the air, like this, like I was swimming, and called out, "Where are my kids? Where are my kids?" and finally they had to tie my arms down on the stretcher, like, well, it was for my protection; I was injured with the concussion.

And when I got to the hospital, I had to have a Barium enema. I had an awful headache, and they wouldn't let me have no aspirin.

I said what the hell you want to give me a Barium enema for when what I got is a headache, but the doctor said he was worried I had a serious ulcer, and he was right: I did, and it was ready to burst or something, so I got to go home and lay in bed for three days, and didn't feel nothing wrong.

But I thought it was so funny, me, waving my arms around like I was swimming: "Where're my kids? Where're my kids?"

SUDDENLY A COMMERCIAL

Y O U!

Yes, YOU!

COULD BE ***IN LOVE!!!***

Tomorrow!!!

It's true! **Experts have Proven**: Seven thousand people in your area will fall in love tomorrow. One of them could be you!

Send just a cash donation of $20.00 today to

CROWCRAFT

2953 Palm Crescent, Abbotsford BC, CANADA V2T 2G5

You will receive **FREE,**

A key word

Which will empower your life

For One Full Year!!!

UNLOCK THE FULL POTENTIAL OF YOUR WORD.

SPECIAL SPECIAL! ***BUY TWO AND SAVE!*** *BUY TEN AND STAY FOR DINNER!*

Buy 100 and receive an interpretive Zen painting.

(VOID WERE PROHIBITED BY LAW.)

EHECATL

Ehecatl (ay HECK atul) was a 'Divine Sweeper.' He worked at Teotihuacan Pyramids in central Mexico, from about 200 B.C. to 700 A.D., but then moved to Mexico City and worked in the pyramids there until Cortes arrived and dismantled the Pyramids and used them to fill in the lake, and then built a Cathedral on top of the whole damn mess, which looked pretty spectacular, but immediately began to sink, and has been sinking ever since.

Ehecatl was no ordinary sweeper: he was a God, and his job was to appear in the form of wind and clean the roads so that Quetzalcoatl (ketsal COE atul) the Feathered Serpent might enter.

In fact, some people say that Ehecatl was a manifestation of Quetzalcoatl himself; when you talked about Quetzalcoatl in his aspect of Divine Wind, you called him Ehecatl.

If you were talking about one particular wind, you would use the name of a different God again, depending on whether the wind was on land, water, before or after rain, or from a particular direction. There were Gods specifically allocated to each type of wind.

Usually, these gods were friendly, always they had a beneficial aspect, but invariably they had certain awesome and terrifying capacities like the need to drink fresh blood or eat a beating heart or cause an earthquake.

It was important to carefully learn the various domains and manifestations in Nature of each God so that you would know which prayers to sing and which special offerings might be required (males would pierce their penis with cactus thorns and offer a few drops of the blood) - whatever was required by the God.

To pay close attention to the weather was to pay close attention to God and to the various manifestations of God, such as the behaviors of plants and birds and animals, the behavior of water, (even just a bowl of water,) and the behavior of wind, and the interconnected behaviors of such visible celestial bodies as the Moon and Venus, (another manifestation of Quetzalcoatl,) and of Mars, and the huge frozen gods in the eyes of the stars.

To pay close attention to Nature was to pray.

WEARY LEATHER SOLACE (for Celeste)

So I had these saddles from sad Jim, and a bunch of other junk crammed into a little flimsy utility trailer.

Boxes of women's clothes, all different sizes: the detritus of daughters.

A broken T.V. that apparently only needed *a new plug for $25.00* and it would be perfectly good (*It was very expensive when I bought it,*) which I gave to my neighbors on condition that I did not get it back. They took it home and plugged it in. It worked great, and they went out and rented two videos that very night; everyone was happy about sad Jim's old T.V. all the next day, but then the next night it died again, so they took it to the junk store.

A preposterous number of curling brooms, many more brooms than would be needed by most teams, entangled with an equally preposterous assortment of excellent badminton rackets, all in well-hinged wooden badminton racket presses.

A bunch of dead badminton cocks, nine pairs of broken boots, a little kid's costume in the shape of a tiger, a few other occasional items like broken lamps and a whole bunch of patterns for dresses, and several neglected answering machines: that was pretty well all he had left after he had sold the house and given away the rest of his marriage.

I traded those saddles for two parrots, which on the whole, I think was a pretty good deal, although saddles don't shit on the floor.

Come to think of it, I must say that all the time I had

them saddles, they weren't nothing but polite.
I kind of miss their weary leather solace.

MOCTEZUMA'S SORROW

People who used to hunt birds, capture them, train them or breed them, or kill them and eat them, and save their feathers, had a particular way of loving birds which we can only wonder about, envy, or tweet grieving bleats to the Twittersphere about.

We prefer photographs. Photographs are in some way better than the originals because you don't remember how pissed off you were that day, and you had a stomach ache. Photographs you can enjoy later when you've got time to look at them.

They say that the Aztecs used to make spectacular sacred wall-hangings of portraits of their Deities by weaving together thousands of carefully chosen feathers.

Their God shimmered.

The most precious feathers were those from around the eyes of the humming-bird, reserved for portraits of the most prominent deities.

Cortes set fire to these feathered creations because they were signs of idolatry.

He wrote*, "This caused Moctezuma and other natives some sorrow."

*(*Quoted from Cortes' letter to his King on reporting his toppling of the Aztec statue of Huitzilpotchli.)*

ON PRONOUNCING THE GODS

HUITZILOPOCHTLI [weet slo POACH tlee], *The Hummingbird God*, gave his people a new identity: "You are no longer Azteca; you are Mexica [meh SHEE kah."]

COATLICUE [kwah TLEE kway] *The Mother Goddess*: her famous huge statue stands out in front of the Museum of Anthropology in Mexico City. This serpent-skirted mother of the War God has two rattlesnakes forming her face, and wears a necklace of freshly-severed human hands and hearts with a skull pendant.

HUITZNAHUA [weets NAH wah] were the many *Brothers of Huitzilopochtli* who joined with his one sister to fight against him. He wanted the people to leave their ancestral home of ATLAN and follow him inland to found a new city, TENOCHTITLAN (Mexico City): just follow the hummingbird until you come to an eagle sitting on a cactus, eating a snake.

COYOLXAUHQUI [koh yohl SHAW kee] is the fearsome *Sister of Huitzilopochtli* who opposed him, and when he defeated her in battle, he cut off her head. A huge basalt carving of her was discovered in 1978, equal in size and power to the STONE OF THE FIFTH SUN, the 'Aztec Calender.'

TEZCATLIPOCA [tess kah tlee POH kah] *Smoking Mirror*: The Original God, patron of the rulers of TENOCHTITLAN. In fact, there were four brothers called Tezcatlipoca, each ruling one of the main compass directions, whose constant interplay of checks and balances kept the world in motion.

NEZAHUALCOYOTL [ness ah wall COH yohtl] was the

Philosopher King in a land of no books: in 1430 he created a wonderful zoo, planted a huge garden of unusual plants, built sophisticated irrigation canals as well as a nine-mile dam for flood control, constructed a 300-room palace, had 40 wives, 60 sons, 57 daughters, and wrote poetry:

Like gold that I cast,

Like jade that I pierce,

Like beads that I string:

That is my song.

MY SADDLES FLEW AWAY

Those two parrots I traded for saddles that flew away came back the next day.

They saw me digging down in the garden, and I think they recognized me and came over to say hello and show off their new wings.

Although they were about eighty feet over my head, in the tops of the birch trees, I could recognize them by their secret flashes of wing-color. However, I had never seen them quite this way before.

I talked to them and asked them to come back, and even placed their cage out in a prominent place, propped the little door open, and rang the bell a few times, but I was pretty sure they wouldn't come back into any cage unless they could bring the birch trees with them.

But they did come back for a visit the day after that; they were in the trees out front this time.

On the third day, my neighbors down the street mentioned waking up to the sounds of parrots in the trees outside their window: they thought they were waking up in Zambia again.

I didn't hear the birds at all yesterday, although I did notice lots of other birds in the air, everybody rushing urgently to Spring.

Haven't heard them today either.

I look up at the birch trees, and I think, Damn: There goes two nice saddles.

WRITHING PAUSE

That woman with the snake on her head refuses to be forgotten.

She has her hands on her hips, but I don't think she is angry: she's just waiting. She's been standing there for quite a while; how many chapters has it been?

She has blue earrings: they could be thin stones, shells, or even feathers. It's hard to tell in clay.

Cobalt blue.

Around her waist is a pale yellow sash supporting a human skull in the center of her body. Her feet are bare; her fingers articulate and intelligent. She looks like a comfortable woman, somebody's aunt: easy to laugh with and easy in her body, fond of writing.

Familiar.

SOMEBODY ELSE WILL MOW THE LAWN

The years, such silent tears.
The leaving-off of ecstasy
And grieving.
Suddenly come
Quick-cut now,
Now.
Snip, tin-snip, the time
Between us.
Go: you're free; it's over.
You don't have to be anyone again.
Somebody else will mow the lawn.
Somebody else will keep an eye on things,
go to work, and fall in love, and have babies
and all that.
They say *I love you.*
They say *I will love you forever.*

RAIN RAINING RAIN

Long ago, in the days when there was still earth on the floor and fire in the sky, people used to have conversations with the rain.

Because of their similar molecular content, people and rain always recognize one another; we feel an affinity for each other's bodies.

Of course, the rain was different in those days: it pronounced actual syllables from an intricate vocabulary of dollop and splash.

Rain would recount long wandering anecdotes explaining why lizards did what they did and the true purpose of arthropods, and they would crack jokes about the weather and about God and pass along news about asteroids.

Sometimes it would be difficult to get the kids to go to bed because they would want to hear the rest of what Rain had to say. Rain would then begin telling a very gently-flowing, now-we-down-going sort of story to please the parents, with lots of s's and whistling noises and softly such sibilance and only occasional glimpses of naked shiny people pounding drums.

Today we still hear the words of the rain but don't know what they mean. Some part of our ancient limbic nervous system has atrophied, like the appendix, or like the ability to wrap ourselves around tree-limbs and, smiling, writhe.

Now, when the rain comes down, it just comes down.

All we hear is rain.

LET'S DO SOMETHING

She got up and moved to the counter.

He picked up a newspaper and began thumbing through it backwards.

She decided to make another batch of pastry.

He began making a list.

She ran her hands down the front of her thighs and found herself inspecting the tile.

He got up and moved purposefully from the table.

She turned and moved purposefully toward the hall.

Their purposes collided.

Such was the tenor of their time together.

Later, each remembered it as Love.

MEDITATION THROUGH BUS WINDOW

I was sitting in a truck. No, not a truck; a bus. A bus-truck.

It seemed at the time that I would be there forever, but I'm not, am I, I'm not still there: leaning an eternity of cold skull against metal window frame, and the vaguely sick feeling that comes from having travelled too far, too soon, too late, and nothing tastes any good any more, a world of stale white sticky buns and Styrofoam coffee, and you don't really know where you are exactly, numbly stupidly staring through the mud-baked window in a glazed coma at a large cardboard box leaning against the wall of wherever, and you think, To hell with it I could just go to sleep there in that box, and let the bus go on without me, but you're too exhausted to move and you would hate to fully wake up and find yourself still just here, in this bus, and anyway, (the thought comes ambling sideways towards you out of the gloom like a drunken horse in a movie theatre,) maybe you are in some part of the world where somebody uses that box and values it very much; in fact maybe that box is Home to somebody, comfortable there beneath the Coca-Cola sign. Maybe that box is a Hilton for someone, used only on special occasions like funerals or circumcisions or trance ceremonies practiced by elderly knowing crones with knives in the dark.

Why don't they shut the fucking motor off? If they shut the motor off, maybe I could get off the bus for just a few minutes and escape that horrible crankcase burning rubber smell, maybe stretch my legs, maybe have a peek inside that box...

Do they ever shut the motors off on buses anywhere in the world?

Maybe the buses come out of the factory already running, and they stay running forever, as long as they are full of people, preferably crammed with people and goats and chickens and bulging with baggage, bicycles and billiard tables and refrigerators roped to the roof-racks; or even just one, just one solitary passenger in a coma, staring blankly through a window glazed with mud, and the bus comes out running, and it just keeps on running, day and night, for years and years and years, until it plunges off some cliff in South America somewhere, and then the big factory doors ooze apart with pneumatic succulence, and another big bus emerges, already running.

Oh, shit; somebody took that box.

REINCARNATION #27: Life as Nothing

I was nothing for an awful long time. How long, I couldn't tell you: I was nothing long before that.

Now, of course, I am not *Nothing*; at the moment, I am this.

Because of that, I cannot imagine Nothing anymore; when I try to remember Nothing, there is just a big blank.

I imagine I was much more comfortable with Nothing than with this. I suspect its lack of shape seemed to suit me. With no time to do anything else, there was always time for Nothing.

Temporary tubes carry Nothing from one way of Being to another.

Inside every molecule is a tiny seed of Nothing just waiting to come out.

Moral: It's the part you can't see that counts.

GOD'S CAFÉ

And then there's the story about the Zen monk who spent twenty years in a cave, eating pine needles and sucking water from stones, who finally gives up in disgust and roars down the hill, determined to order a pizza.

He goes into a restaurant and sits down, but just at that very moment, as he looks into the menu, he experiences the perfect *satori:* earth-shattering, nerve-shivering bliss.

Eventually, the man dies, but THE MENU remains, tucked away in some old box somewhere, or maybe it's enshrined already.

Then some scholar, some erstwhile seeker after truth, seeks it out and irons the wrinkles out of it and sneaks it under his shirt, and takes it home to America or Germany or Norway and makes ten thousand copies of it in order to share it with the rest of the world, maybe make a few dollars: publish a book, make a tape, give a workshop.

Pretty soon, thousands of people will have copies of THE MENU, tens of thousands. They mail away for them or get them free in grocery bags and at government campsites; they nail them up on their walls and put vases of flowers below them – or maybe just ritually sucked rocks.

Some people memorize THE MENU in its entirety and present oral recitations at Weddings and Bar Mitzvahs; others use THE MENU as an oracle: they throw sucked stones upon it and read the covered words. Diets change, menus change, restaurants flourish; THE MENU is sung, chanted, intoned, inhaled, exhaled, exhumed, and adored in mangers; THE MENU is eaten.

Finally, the MENU becomes God.

And God says, OK, you may place your order now, but remember:

Service is *Slow...*

TEN FOR DAN

Dan was a prick.

He was born that way, and he stayed that way. When he died, people said, Too bad about Dan, but he was a kind of a prick, don't you think?

His wife knew, even when she married him, that he was a prick. She didn't think the kids would find out, at least not as soon as they did, but they did.

Even the dog thought Dan was a prick.

I would like to tell you there was one redeeming feature in Dan's life, just one magic gesture that he managed to perform, which reduced all the rest of his persistently pricky doings to an inconsequential back-drop.

But there really wasn't.

Dan was just a prick.

Through and through.

ON ARTISTS AND DRYWALLERS

The duty of the artist is to create: to create is to act on faith, to do a gratuitous act that has no apparent value beyond the pleasure of bringing into being.

Unfortunately, artists need cigarettes: being sensitive souls, they are the ones who embraced most enthusiastically the government-sponsored fifty-year worldwide advertising campaign that promoted smoking as a means of finding momentary release from the stresses of life and as an alternative to food, which was in short supply at the time.

Money was invented so that artists could buy cigarettes. It would have been much simpler if the government had just given cigarettes free to the artists, but then everyone would have wanted to be an artist, and the government would have had to lay off hundreds of thousands of people whose jobs it is to collect cigarette taxes so that they can give the money to cigarette companies in the form of income tax write-offs and subsidies for farm machinery.

Besides, it is dangerous to have too many artists because a country that has too many artists always has a revolution sooner or later, and we couldn't have that: a whole bunch of artists running the country, each one with different ideas of ownership and regulations (*Who gets the parking meter money*, and *Where shall we put the garbage?)*

So it is safer to increase the taxes on cigarettes because then all the artists and other dreamers will become preoccupied with getting enough money together to buy cigarettes and will never get organized enough to prepare a sound artistic alternative to the world of taxes and cigarettes.

And so the artist becomes a drywaller or installer of sundecks or a designer of windows, but of course, is never really happy because there is forever an unfinished creature, a defrosted painting, or an un-sung song going moldy in the back of the refrigerator.

People are always suspicious of unhappy drywallers, and rightly so because unhappy drywallers are a notoriously dangerous and ill-mannered brood.

So the artist doesn't get much work and spends more and more time in darkened rooms, yearning for a Marlboro sunrise.

After they are dead, somebody else gets the art.

MOVING PICTURES IN THE HEAD

Many long years ago, there were no roads to anywhere, so everyone pretty much stayed home. They did a lot of dreaming in those days and got a lot of pleasure from watching the moving pictures in their head.

Suddenly they invented roads, and everyone felt that they really ought to leave their homes and just go somewhere, anywhere (Look: we can go over there!)

Those who didn't want to go somewhere were looked down on as timid, unimaginative, and dull; pretty soon, everyone was on the road somewhere.

But it got tiring carrying around sleeping bags and pots and pans and toilet paper and coloring books and dream pictures painted on stones, so somebody had the idea to find some use for all these empty houses that were sitting around here; maybe we'll just stay here for a little while, maybe we'll have a baby or something.

Then somebody invented the News on Television, and now there was no longer any reason to leave the house because you could find out everything right there. In fact, if you went outside, you might miss something.

You might suppose that now people would finally be Happy, but no.

What they had on television ,in between all the pictures of the bus-train collisions, exploding airplanes, and leaking nuclear waste barrels floating in the Gulf of Mexico, were pictures of thousands of new and fresh and wonderful things you could buy: there were speed-boats, and airplanes, and hang-gliders, and dirigibles, and rare tomato seeds, and things to unplug your sink, and step-by-step videos that will show you how to become rich, and secrets of skin regeneration, and tiny computers, all of which you could BUY RIGHT NOW, using this special 1-800 number, (please have your credit card ready), and foreign language courses, and free samples of valve lubricant, and essential oils, and kitchen scales that could weigh a single gram of fat-free yogurt.

Any single one of these things seemed so much to be preferred over the little moving pictures in the head and no roads at all.

REINCARNATION # 63: Life as a Porcupine

Life among the porcupines was prickly, of course, but when you are born into a state of prickliness and learn how to eat and love and die while prickly, you tend to regard prickliness with much more equanimity than those accustomed to less prickly environments.

It's like the situation we have with *Silence*: we call it Silence, but really we are in the midst of a colossal racket as the ever-exploding universe sings its uni-verse to us, to the tune of billions of atomic bombs per day in our astral vicinity, and we, we don't even notice it; we call it Silence.

The Ancient Greeks used to say that each planet, as it whirls its path through the void, makes a sort of humming or deep whistling noise, the way things do when you spin them.

Because they are all moving at different speeds and are of different masses, they hum different notes, and since their distances from one another also vary, there is also a constant fluctuation in tone and volume within each sound.

The combined effect of all this planetary humming is called "The Music of the Spheres": a whole octave being hummed everywhere in the universe.

The reason we can't hear it is that we were born into it, and we had never known a single second when that sound was not there, and we die into that silence still hearing it.

So it is with prickliness: it doesn't necessarily have to bother you. You might never notice it; you might even come to love it.

Still, in the morning, your eyes would open.
Still, in the evening, they would close.

ON NOT TAKING HEROIN

I have never taken Heroin, and I don't think I will.

I took a whole whack of Morphine one time by mistake, in the hippie days, you know, with two strange but pretty girls I had just met, on a big bed, who knew a psychiatrist I also knew, who traded them certain medicines for certain favors, I was told, as we smoked a joint together on this big old brass bed, in a quaint little hotel on Davie street, window over the street: the kind of place you would never have noticed if you walked by outside; it had always been there, with courtly rooms, and old furniture, and windows that would open, and a dining room with regular guests, and regular hours, where I now sat ogling the cutlery, staring dumbfounded at nonchalant plates that wobbled and warped, while man-size amoebas detached themselves from wallpaper.

It all started with my headache: I used to get migraines about once a month in those days, and I could feel one coming on, and I didn't want to ruin the party, so I asked the girls if they happened to have a 292 or other strong headache pills, and they said they had something better than that for headaches, in fact, they were the very best pills for headaches, which they got from this doctor, and I could have one: in fact, here, take two, ...which of course turned out to be industrial strength Morphine.

I couldn't deal with the amoebas in the wallpaper anymore, but I didn't dare go back to their room with them, so I decided to leave.

It took 45 minutes to develop the proper co-ordination

to cross the street: big-lit Davie Street on a noisy Saturday night, with multi-dimensional buses bursting forth from vastly improbable directions and huge tunnels that kept appearing in the air: beckoning, inviting, singing, and wobbling there.

And then I drove my car! It seems preposterous now: whirring cosmic vortexes off the front fender; mysterious doors and tunnels, bridges in the air; the secret intentions of engines; an inability to precisely recall the mechanics involved in such fundamental maneuvers as "Turn."

Whole worlds and planes of light collided with my eyes, revealing days the dinosaurs would recognize: ancient and relentless, magnificent maelstrom: until the charging light of night retreated with the morning sky, and the first few clouds in the east burst forth original Day, again, for me, at the shore of the sea.

Me, at the beach, welded onto the wheel of my '52 Chev, willing the sun to come up, willing my variously sundered cosmic parts back from the far-flung corners of the galaxy, so I could tend to my more immediate functions like breathing and the integration of my eyes with this world of imponderable gravity, intersection, and perpendicularity . . .

And headaches, Christ.

No, I'll stay away from Heroin.

ON BANGING DOORS

Never listen to a banging door. Banging doors have been known to reverberate for thousands of years, and people who listen to them often go crazy and die believing that the sound of banging doors is what silence is.

When a door bangs shut, as they do, as they do, try to ignore it. Try to stem the sudden rush of panic in the heart: try to behave as you would if it were just the sound of any door closing in an ordinary way.

On occasion, the door is banged shut so hard that the latch doesn't even have time to react, and the door bangs open again, bouncing off the frame, and you must endure two violent bangs of air right between the eyes, and now the third time the door half-closes again, ironically, slowly, savoring your distress, while the sound of the door, double-banging, Geminis your consciousness into eccentric jangling oscillation.

Sometimes, and these are worst of all, the sound of the door slamming is a huge and masterful hammering that leaves you floundered on the floor while no actual door has been shut at all.

The ordinary door stands implacably before you, and you hate it, because now there is a huge relentless portcullis whammed shut in front of you, between you and that person sitting . . . just over there, only now the sound of banging doors whams your eyes to Kingdom fucking come.

So sudden. So brutal.

So gone.

ON THE FUTILITY OF SPEECH

There is no point in saying anything because you can never say exactly what you mean. There is always at least one color or flavor in the words which is personal to you alone; the sum experience of all your moments up to this one.

The biggest contributor to color or personal tone of voice is, of course, what we call the Ego. Therefore the Zen masters live in silence and perform the most elegant, eloquent vocabularies of Tea, Archery, and Kendo.

But we, alas, are not Zen masters, and we have to go to Safeway, and can you imagine getting your change and not at least saying something to somebody, at least saying Thank-you when you get your card back: it would be rude, and, besides, I like to talk.

Nonetheless, I suppose we could at least talk less. Talk less, and intend more.

Writing it out can help: it is one thing to think you know what you think, and quite another thing to try writing it down, especially when what you think you know has to do with the sound of one hand clapping or "the ineluctable modality of the visible."

When you examine your writing, especially when it's typed up cold on the page, you can see more clearly the faults in your thinking, the parts of "you" that are intruding into the clarity of the idea.

(Oh, Jaysus, I'm doing it again...)

THE FUTILITY OF SPEECH: PART 2

The trouble is, once you get it through your thick skull that most of what you say out loud is just... mouthwash, mealy froth, mumble-jumble, and you finally learn to keep your mouth shut, at least for two or three minutes at a time, and *listen* first, or at least *think*, then you begin to see more and more clearly how most of what everybody says is just idle word-mumble, too.

And so we come to the voices in the head.

Every human being who manages to live enough years to become what is called *old* must spend a lot of time, at least at the end of those years, say the last fifteen or twenty, thirty maybe, listening to the voices in the head; sometimes listening to them, sometimes talking to them.

The voices in front don't matter so much anymore.

I used to visit my grandmother, my sweet Nana, in her hospital bed at the Extended Care ward out at UBC. She shared a room with three other old ladies, all of whom were dying more than she was.

Instead of feeling depressed about it, she looked for opportunities to enter an intentionally contemplative state, such as before she entered the day formally by getting into her wheelchair.

During that time, from about 4:00 a.m. to 7:30 a.m., as she was waiting for somebody to come and help her get up (because she couldn't reach down to put her slippers on, or get into her wheelchair), she would just lie there, with her eyes half-shut, and let her mind open to God in general, and then to the Angels, and finally to any visitors they might want to bring along.

She would watch the scenes unroll without interfering, sometimes replaying the role of her own years: 10 years ago already since last weaving on her loom; 20 years ago her dying son; 30 years ago her dying husband; 40 years ago the war; 50 years ago the little house in Steveston; 60 years ago Migod Mary at Manson's Landing; 70 years ago birthing babies in the homestead cabin; 80 years ago her Wedding day; 90 years ago hunch-back Tom in Ireland crying Goodbye; 100 years ago, now, here, with the Angels by her bed.

God doesn't talk, you know, she said to me one day; *But he talked to me.*

ANYWHERE AGAIN (A Song, for Ed)

I'm hungry and horny,
And broke as a bitch.
Bring lovin' or cigarettes,
It doesn't matter which.
Would someone please tell me why hours
Keep coming (and coming and coming)
And I just sit gazing,
At wave after wave.
It's crazy, I know it,
I can't help but show it.
But people look sideways,
And pass me quite quickly
(I'm foreign or dirty or
Likely quite sickly.)
I think it is true
You can talk to the angels,
And listen to voices
And not feel so lonely.
But stretches of time left
Their traces are all over
Your faces, your lines, all
Your lives out the door.

And sooner or later,
You're back in the bedroom,
With silence and spiders,
And songs out of tune.
Those dancers and lovers,
And people who lingered
With shadows at twilight:
Such delicate fingers.
Time takes you
Quite knowing
You'll never
Be going
Any
Where
Again.

CHAPTER FORTY-TWO

When Marilyn Monroe became bored with being Marilyn Monroe, as most people do, she changed her name to Jean Shrimpton and moved to Des Moines, Iowa.

Most people in Des Moines, Iowa are waitresses. When they get tired of being waitresses they become hairdressers.

But usually they go back to being waitresses because the tips are better. Especially if they do their customers' hair while serving them coffee.

Booth people get their hair done. Counter people, just their nails.

There are no men in Des Moines, Iowa. It is a rather peculiar place, and you might want to reconsider going there. Unless you take your hair with cream and sugar.

THOSE WERE THE MOMENTS

Sorrow tore the order

From the tired waiter's hands,

And threw it on the floor.

It wasn't bad enough that he had to write the stupid thing down; now he had to get down on his hands and knees and crawl around underneath the table with chewing gum and spiders and moldy silences in order to fulfil it.

Life's like, that, thought Carle grimly as he eyed the wide mouth of the old wood stove.

Climbing into that would be so much simpler than just about anything else he could think of right now.

But no, not this time.

Back to days and ways, huh, Carle?

At least I had those moments,

with um... Sylvia,

he muttered, getting up,

making his way through the double swinging doors.

Those were moments.

Those were moments.

Clubhouse: toasted.

ON DYING

Every day a little bit.

Do anything a little bit, every day, all your life, and after a time, you get pretty good at it.

Like loving, for instance, or eating pizza, or dying, now that you mention it.

We all die with the same score, 100% dead; nonetheless, some of us manage to do it with a little more grace than others, more elegance. These are the ones who have practiced the longest.

If you and I want to be when our turn comes (everybody gets a turn), one of those old people who are buoyant, and still friendly, still a source of light and warmth to others, approaching Death gently, almost with affection, then we have to start practicing Now; it's not one of those things you can Panic Cram.

Everybody takes this test; everybody fails. So why do it in a dim room bound to a big white bed, howling torment bloody Mommy?

Let us go with felicity,

And calm,

And a little melody

Still playing in the head.

Shall we dance?

HOWLING IN BLACK AND WHITE

Love tore the silences from me, breached
The cloak and fabric,
Left me, mother-
Shudder naked,
To uncover once again, me:
I am still here.
I can do anything I want.

My grandmother used to say that one of the advantages of being very old was that you could literally do anything you wanted at any time. People would have to put up with it, like you suddenly singing in a Chinese restaurant, or insisting that the tea be hotter, throwing the table-arrangement flowers on the floor, or maybe just quietly sitting there and eating them.

Everyone would have to excuse you because you're just so damn old now: you can't help it, and besides, you can’t even hear them if they complain at you.

But how about when I am only as old as I am now – could I get away with it?

Could I go out in my driveway, roll around in the mud puddles, take my clothes off, and howl madly about the treachery of traffic lights, the iniquities of electrical conduits, the inevitable betrayal of grasses and leaves?

It could get awkward;
I might want to speak to those neighbors again,
Might want to borrow their trailer.

Better to leave my trousers trussed,
Write poetry:
This very private madness.
Howling in black and white.

LATER

I miss you.
I miss you ruined roses,
Dozens of damned dalmatian dahlias.
I miss you cavalcades of convulvus,
Hysteria of wisteria.
I miss your fucking socks.
How cruel that you left your sweatpants behind.
Now I can't use that drawer anymore:
You are still in there,
Changing or something.
My hallway mirror
Looks for you.
I think I finally got the last of your hair
Out of the bathtub drain.
I found that pot-lid.
What am I supposed to do
With all this lard?

RIPPLES

As the pond
Rippled, so did I.
Past these moments,
Past the times that used to be,
The times of you and me.
Now rippling,
We come together again at the edges,
Familiar.
Time warps out beyond our memory of us.
Ripples remain.
The ripples were always so.
The ripples were always.
The ripples were.
The ripples.
The.

AND THEN ANOTHER MORNING CAME

And then another morning came.
It's me,
I'm here again,
I wasn't sure I would be.
So what to do.
This business is called Getting Up.
How old I am today.
Let me see,
That's what we say,
And then we see:
Rivers rising, flooding backward
Swollen banks, houses trembling, toppling;
Doors unlocking, un-releasing, un-re-locking, locks
Quite apart; treasures untreasured, alas,
Or the wrong treasures treasured:
Oh well, it's a treasure, isn't it?
All of this on the intake of a breath:
Split-second sideways
Boundless fathoms, chasms
Of voices, times, and tender touches
To get lost in, before, before,
Before you answer, finally,

Fine, Thanks, Great,

You?

And spun off flying, eyeing sideways, terrified with wonder and with beauty and with all the loving you could muster: 10 years, 20, 30, 40, 50 years;

Later, finally, eighty.

I did love you,

Will love you,

Forever.

And then another morning came.

ODE FOR WEEPING BIRCH

One day the bulldozers appeared and ripped down all the trees.

They didn't even bother to saw them down first, just crunch crunch, smash chew, throw them in the chipper, without anybody knowing what to do about it; nobody was really sure whose bulldozers they were, and anyway, who was going to walk into a muddy field and get mad at a bunch of big bulldozers?

Sorry, I missed that neighborhood meeting, but I was really busy. I'll be there next time for sure.

Which trees did they rip out? Over there?

No, there are no trees over there; that's Hazelwood Heights.

Really nice condos, upper end, you know, 2800 square feet, low 900’s.

Landscaped, too: nice mulch.

Seen the weeping birch?

ON TALKING WITH ANGELS

Angels sing, of course; it is very natural for them.

They don't mind if you listen; they know that it is pretty unlikely that you will understand what they are singing, so if you want to cast your ear there or there, just so, it's all right with the angels. So you can listen if you want.

You can tap your fingers or whistle along under your breath while you while you wait for the light to change.

Whether you can get the angels to talk to you is quite another matter and one which is dependent upon how diligently and how delicately you pursue them.

Angels do not like to be pursued; let us not forget: they prefer a more subtle, more indirect seduction.

They prefer singing to any kind of talking, anyway: and they sing in another language called Ecstasy.

So if you presume to be familiar enough with the angels to expect them to talk to you, or to acknowledge you, then you must learn to sing to them in their own language.

You have to pursue them ardently, listening closely, for many years; watching for them passionately, with the blind devotion of any lover...

While not appearing to do so.

So they sing.

ON SINKING INTO OCEANS

Because of the sadness surrounding her, or at least so she said; (it may not have been that way at all, of course, but she, but she said it was so, and so it was so:) because of that, wave after wave, inexhaustible oceans tumbling towards her, every time: every time she opened her eyes, they were there, right before her eyes, in front of her, tumbling huge, and hungry maws and jaws surround her.

Because of that (or so she said, as I said) because of that, every color, every nuance, every ounce of every day was quite squeezed dry with doom; sooner or later, around the edges of any moment (and sooner, far sooner than seemed fair, in fact,) each moment groaned, swollen, too tender to be touched by other moments, moments gone; gone, gone so far was even frequently forgotten gone, and only blind photographs of yesterday's dumb camera left lingering shape of gesture and of form upon the pillow to remind her.

Because of this little demon on her shoulder poking pitchforks, grinning gristly jokes to quite confounding her, found her flapping backward, so sudden cod upon the dock, belly heaving, heavy, yearning turning terrible air back, again, just once, oh gulp, oh sweetly please, just once again, let me, let me go, before I go wherever air will have me: how strange this sudden shape I find myself, now floundered; flat and dying once again.

Because of this huge world with no room for her - room for rivers, doubtless, room for oceans, mountains, trees and yes, alas, airplanes and industrial machinery and roads but no, no room for her, here, her here: her neighbors didn't like to say hello to her, they turned their heads a little at the supermarket; no room for her in Superstore when everybody else had a cart and a purpose and could tell you whether 2.92 kg. was good, whether in fact it meant anything at all, or was just there, like those strange numbers you see on smokestacks of battleships in old World War 1 newsreels, plunging savage oceans, grey on grey.

Because of this, as I said, this terrible reverberation of everybody gesture that pervaded her invaded her through thorns upon the table of her childhood: mommy manners make me miss my meat; funny teeth to smile with, keep away; stupid peas and forks; silly brother sister squabbles played out forty years later, going strong, and thrived upon one knife-wise; the inevitable solace of hidden by-ways even then; even then, the spiders beneath the stairs could tell who she was.

And so the moment's sudden loss; no sweetness to this tea, no matter how many times I try to remember, the first few times I loved you so, and tasted so, then, now become another tin to open, another package to undo, another bag another way, another day, any other day would do, then this, she mused, idly clunking the kitchen cupboard shut with her knee; just so, not hard enough to hurt her knee, (so many ways,) nor so hard to make a noise, (why shouldn't she make a noise? but anyway, she didn't,) nor so soft the cupboard should not shut; not this, nor that, but so, even so, and just this way, again, and again and again: correct.

And so the fear of mirrors, and the unquenchable need for them, a hundred times a day, if possible: glimpses in windows, and traces in puddles, and passing strangers' eyes; even just a dog, sometimes, just to check: am I really here, this moment, and if I am, how could I be, and how can I not know my body anymore, and is that not me just around the corner, and will I recognize myself in dreams, and am I finally happy, then, is that what this is?

And so the solitude of kitchens and the solace of set sequence: the certainty of bread; the ritual of boiling water; the particular arrangement of the head upon pillow; the arrangement of hair; the touch of self that only lonely knows; the turn of a page, as pages read themselves to sleep upon your breast; words merge into mind, and memories of other people's dreams, when only the two of you were, and you could, and you did, glistening afterward, thinking, There, I did it, I did: I had some happiness; I'm pretty sure that's what that was.

Down, down, down again, down drowning draws dark night: magnet call of gravity commands your heart to pump, keep, pump again, pump, keep..., sleep perhaps is coming, don't you know,

By dreaming dragons drowsy-drawn, here,

This ancient cave,

And in the night, sweet pictures cast perchance upon your walls

And little calls of love to linger by,

With names you never knew,

Before relaxing your rage and cleanly little bones and veins, remember.

Sunk:

My ship is down,

My oars have gone

The ocean disembodied:

Everything happened
So fast.

STARS FOR SHEILA

Sheila like stars. She could remember being outside on her grandfather's farm in Nakusp when she was not quite two years old, and being lifted up in his arms and suddenly thrust head-first into this huge vista of stars, as if her head had been stuck through some membrane on the other side of ordinary night, and her whole head was huge with stars, and it never could be any other way, and she was stuck numb and dumb with their huge cold twinkling certainty.

They carried her into the house then and put her in a nice puffy bed, but the stars but the stars did no go away, could not go away, never did go away even now, right now, they were there, or at least some distant reverberation of them, like Balouch rug designs echoing the pyramids.

Then she met Larry. Larry lived in Langley, and drove trucks. When he could get work, that is: he couldn't often get it. Then he went to northern Alberta and couldn't get it there either. But he never came back: *Well what the fuck, might as well not get it here. Or maybe I'll go to the Northwest Territories, and not get it there neither.*

Meanwhile Sheila had a son named Jamie who was four years old but would not speak. But every time he stood near a train going by he would rush his hands to his ears and thrust this huge rush of train-gush joy noise from his solar plexus, and millions and millions of stars would tumble out of his mouth, cascading all over Sheila, all over her life and everything she ever did or said or thought about.

ON ANGELS AND WASHING MACHINES

On Saturday, the sullen angels did my laundry: on Sunday, they wouldn't have anything to do with me. That's the price you pay when you aspire to celestial company.

At least they help with the laundry. I guess everyone who has a connection with angels is able to benefit from them in some tangible way.

Some people, for example, seduce, or at least cajole, the angels into letting them become incredible dancers: ice dancers especially, but even talk show hosts, or preparers of preposterous puddings; with me, it's laundry.

The angels don't seem to give a shit about my Mastercard bill. They glance askance as the transmission in my van grinds its gears to the gum line. Neither are they interested in interspersing any magical interventions into my autistic artistic career.

The house falls to ruin about my knees, but this bleak, bloody washing machine that I bought second-hand and died eleven years ago just keeps on whirring and working.

Moral: Failing nirvana, there is still some value in angels.

SOON PERHAPS A SHIFT

What is this thing called Ecstasy? One minute you are in it, sweet soaring, and the next minute down on your knees with greasy wrenches or queasy wenches or steely benches, and then, and then and then and then... ah, yes, sweet, that, one moment again.

It sounds like being in Love, doesn't it? And I suppose it is, only Being, with no object and no subject, just *Being*, in *Love*

With a certain shift of light yesterday, the young hemlock outside my window glowed vibrantly in two very distinct hues of green. I could see exactly the electric urging of all the new growth on the tips of the branches: the tree was alive and gloriously pulsing with energy and intention.

It reminded me of a young man who needs his first shave: I wanted to go out there and shave that Hemlock.

Later the light shifted, and the tree was just one color again: green, a tree in an ordinary way. And now, this morning, just one color again: green, as you might expect.

Soon, perhaps, a shift of light.

ON GODS AND SILENT SPAGHETTI

I don't trust Gods with big grins on their faces. Gods don't need to smile. God is enough.

Gods are not interested in ordinary happiness: they are dazed and dynamited with the bliss of being.

BE! BE! BE! they cry, and we, and we, and we tag along after, tapping our toes in time, humming a little song, some of us driving Mazdas.

All the Gods care about is that everything that can be, *will* be, and RIGHT NOW, and ALL AT ONCE, PLEASE!

The Gods are cosmic cheerleaders with razzle-dazzle death pom-poms and comfortable fat snakes on their heads.

It is only incidental to these arcane conjectures that I admit to you that when I create gods, I can't manage to make them smile: even when I try, by the time they dry, they end up with a kind of knowing smirk as if they know something that I don't.

It is what I do, you see: I make faces and heads of Gods, which end up hanging about in my kitchen, where they can bear silent witness to my relationship with. . . spaghetti.

I'll take my gods grim, thanks very much: smiling witnesses to silent spaghetti would be too much to bear.

THE BIG FEAR

Everybody knows The Big Fear.

It's the axe in the night, the burst of blood in the brain, and one stupid fucking stumble in the driveway.

One way to ignore The Big Fear is to talk energetically, enthusiastically, and often. Many people do this.

You can memorize lists, ordered information, and donuts for the mind, like recipes, hockey scores or stock market quotations, or the marital status of Rock Stars. Many people do this.

Another way to hold off The Big Fear is to sit in darkened rooms and hold very still and speak only seldom, and then only quietly, to yourself, the ticking of the clock, viewing the world from computers and televisions and sheltered windows. Many people do this.

Nevertheless: Oh God, I'm dying, Honey.

Remember me.

BACK IN A MINUTE

Which door is this: is this where I came in? Could we back it up a little to where I took that turn, somewhere back there: where was it?

I knew it was a one-way street, but I thought I could deke around and go through the alley somehow.

I really believe that those girls I talked to thirty, thirty-five years ago, forty-five, fifty-five years, my god, must still be there, beneath the streetlights, leaning against the long light, laughing with each other, making little shrieks.

Trouble is they took down those old streetlights, took away the whole damn street, built mountains of monoliths, towers, and townhomes, and condo blocks, so those leaning girls with the leaping eyes and miles of smiles and silky scents and bow-down flowers now bowed down there beneath the asphalt in the parking lot. So I would have to bring a wheelbarrow, shit, bring twenty-five wheelbarrows and a dump truck, and hold up traffic for a couple of weeks, saying, Hold on a minute: I just wanna talk to these girls.

They were right around here somewhere.

Listen: can't you smell them?

If I could find my old telephone book, I could still phone them up using the old numbers, and they would still answer with the same old voices, the same laughter.

I never said goodbye.

THE BUDDHA'S CARPET

Ted wanted a certain carpet that he had been looking at for a while, hanging on the wall of the carpet store in the local Bazaar, and finally, after months of looking at it and thinking about it, he scraped enough Rupees together and went to buy it, only to discover that The Buddha had already bought it, just last Tuesday.

Damn: Ted really wanted that carpet.

Nobody wants to steal a carpet from The Buddha; I mean, even if you don't really believe it, do you want to risk Bad Karma for a thousand more existences just for the sake of a lousy carpet to put down on the floor of your hovel?

Maybe his karma would be to be a rug dealer for all those ten thousand existences, locked behind barred windows with expensive alarms and moth-killing chemicals.

And he couldn't buy the carpet from the Buddha because The Buddha had no use for money.

The Buddha said if he had any money, the only thing he could think of doing with it right at the moment was buying a carpet, and since he already had a carpet then . . . (he shrugged his shoulders.)

He suggested that maybe Ted wait until he got tired of the carpet, and then Ted could have it for nothing.

However, it was hard to imagine getting tired of it in the near future because it was serving a useful purpose at this time.

So it could be a while, Ted said.

Mmm, said The Buddha.

Aah, said Ted.

STORIES IN FOUR SENTENCES

ICE-CREAM SATORI

A little while ago, a little girl watched in horror as the whole top part of her ice cream cone leaped away from the top of her cone and went splat onto hot asphalt with ants and engine oil and an old man's spit.

It was the most violent, shocking thing that had ever happened to her in her whole life up to that moment.

All she had left was a little bit of ice cream around the edges of the cone, but it tasted like tragedy, and she refused to eat it.

At this moment, the asphalt bears a pink-sugar smudge in the shape of a lip.

"HAMLET, THOU HAST CLEAV'D MY HEART"

Sorrow cleaved her; it didn't just cut her; there is a difference.

When sorrow just cuts you, it's not so bad; you can go on, like the kid who skins a knee and runs in crying Mommy.

Not so the sorrow which cleaves: this one makes you swallow hot coals from the barbecue.

This one makes the whole numb world go dumb.

REINCARNATION #72: Life As a Lizard.

The really wonderful thing about my life as a lizard was the amount of time we spent practicing invisibility, or at least the form of invisibility (that word with five eyes) based on immobility and an outward blending of the body with the environment: I could look like a shadow on a rock for hours.

The unfortunate aspect of this skill is that it ensured a very solitary existence because we were continually losing one another, sometimes for hours, sometimes for days, sometimes for months, sometimes forever, as we mistook one another for shadows, or for food, or for another stick for the fire at night - YIKES: There goes, Uncle Henry!

I shouldn't be facetious; on the whole, I am glad for that training. It is so useful now, in this form and in this time, to be able to hold still, and to wait, patiently: becoming one with stones and sticks and trees, for hours, for days, for months, forever.

LOVE AT THE LAUNDROMAT

Time washing.
Time is washing us.
Double rinse cycle.
We'll be finished together.

REINCARNATION #87: Life as a Butterfly

Life, as a butterfly, was,
Such another matter, such an
Other matter, such an
Another other matter,
Me, more, now, how:
Take a break.

All I knew was fragrant air,
And wings and singing living things and,
Restless, winds, sometimes, and,
Rain:
A break.

Aztec air exhaling colored snow,
In Spring, take wing, take,
Urgent huge hot soft,
Butter-quiet,
Transparent wings,
Against thy cheek, my love,
My velvet light:
Break.
And to return to seed with warm

Wings wrapped in mummy larval
Branches, so bushy babies eat me
Inside out come Spring again,
White, see: sweet, bare, air, continues...
Take.

ON NOT ARGUING WITH ZEBRAS

Zebras are temperamental, querulous beasts with whom it is tedious to argue.

I once argued with a Zebra from the fall of 1952 until after the change in the model year for 1958, which was when the Chevy got that big set of boxy tail-lights; we argued every day from dawn to dusk except for the 17th of February, and still, we could not agree on a simple YES or NO.

Before we could agree on YES or NO, we had to discuss SHOULD or SHOULD NOT, and all the moral implications in between, starting with Euripides, for convenience, but back tailing to an asteroid impact before finally getting waylaid by Al Capone; then we had to take into consideration WOULD or WOULD NOT, which got us side-tracked into the slipstream of neurology and genetics and the price of copper futures, which naturally evolved to COULD and COULD NOT, which sometimes depend on the number of, or indeed the presence of, vertebrae, the quality of the coffee, and anyway: What if you had a headache?

At the end of our time together, that zebra was no more enlightened than before.

SHIT SATORI

Yeah, but what I mean is.

No, but what I meant was, like, well, yeah, you know.

Let me put it this way.

Shit.

REINCARNATION #93: Life as a Penguin

Contrary to what you might expect, life among the penguins was not blissful.

There were only two things to do: sit around the house watching T.V., or go to the singles bar, to drink Shirley Temples and smoke low-tar cigarettes, or, three, make love in one way or another.

Sorry, wrong picture: that should read, stand around on the ice, jump into the freezing water to eat cold fish, or make love in one way or another.

So: much the same.

FOUR FOR NANA

Yes, and yes, the mysteries of her, the storybooks of her eyes, and of her hair, and of her, there, just her.

How many times I watched her, how many days and ways I knew her finally, and then, at last, forever.

I knew those things once also,

Said she, wheel-chair windowed,

To herself, mostly because,

Because because,

There was no one left to say them to, alas.

And so the touch of air upon hair,

So the slow sea moan;

So the rising tide within me singing rain and stringing gypsies in the sunlight of our time:

Sweet days, flower-fallen,

Come to this,

And the memory of this.

Available for Readings, Performances, and Workshops:
Spoken Word, Written Word, and Making Creatures.

tonyrekert@gmail.com

About the Author

Tony Rekert lives in the Fraser Valley of British Columbia, Canada. His backyard provides nesting for 2 species of woodpeckers, a flock of chickadees, two pairs of nuthatches, a family of hummingbirds, and three raccoons in the cedar tree.

He worked as an English teacher - in Junior High, Senior High, Prison, and College – until he retired from full-time work at age 38 in order to consider life as poetry.

He supported himself by selling hand-made artifacts from India and Nepal, and for 15 years, he traveled annually to those countries to search for inventories. He had a store on eBay during those years, specializing in Singing Bowls. During the summer, he would load up his van and set it up at outdoor markets; in winter, sell it on the eBay store.

These days he is "concentrating on loose ends" and preparing to downsize and move a bit further into the country. One loose end was to get this little manuscript published, which in one way or another, has been fermenting in various notebooks for a couple of decades.

Dolly Dobbyn was his grandmother (1886-1988).

Manufactured by Amazon.ca
Bolton, ON

32362745R00072